Alphabet Trains

Samantha R. Vamos

Illustrated by **Ryan O'Rourke**

A B C D E F G H I J K L M N O P Q R S T U V W X Y Z

Charlesbridge

Tear the ticket.
Load the freight.
Sound the whistle.
Raise the gate.

Clank! Chug-chug! Whoosh!

Alphabet trains.

A is for Auto Train.
Load your car on the rack.

B is for bullet train—
high speed on welded track.

C is for coal train,
carting coal from a mine.

D is for dinky train,
a short railroad line.

E is for elevated train,
cruising on raised tracks.

F is for freight train,
hauling goods piled in stacks.

G is for Glacier Express,
a scenic, alpine glide.

H is for Hurricane Turn.
Wave a flag to catch a ride.

I is for incline train,
a steep, uphill track.

J is for Jupiter,
with a wide balloon stack.

K is for Komet,
traveling through the night.

L is for Leonardo Express—
a trip to Rome postflight.

M is for monorail, a wider train on just one rail.

N is for narrow-gauge train.
Train and track are smaller scale.

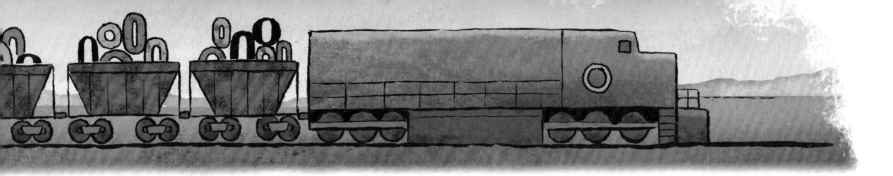

O is for ore train,
hauling iron in the back.

P is for Pacific Surfliner.
Store your surfboard on a rack.

Q is for Q train–
Fifth to Lex in record time.

R is for Rocky Mountaineer,
a sea-to-sky climb.

S is for snowplow train.
Its blades carve
through the snow.

T is for top-and-tail train—
forward, backward, to and fro!

U is for unit train—
one freight to one location.

V is for Victoria Express,
a Vietnam destination.

W is for wilderness train,
a wildlife tour on rails.

X is for Xplorer,
a trip through New South Wales.

Y is for Yellow Train.
Up the mountains it goes!

Z is for California Zephyr.
Book a sleeper car and doze.

Around the world,
from land to sea,
trains work hard
from A to Z.

Clank!
Chug-chug!
Whoosh!

Alphabet trains.

Amtrak's **Auto Train** transports passengers and vehicles between Virginia and Florida. Vehicles ride in freight cars called auto racks.

Bullet trains are named for their shape and speed. Their tracks are smooth so the trains move quickly. Japan's Shinkansen trains are some of the fastest bullet trains in the world.

A **coal train** transports coal from a mine to a utility company or other destination.

A railroad line with a short track and train is sometimes called a **dinky train**. New Jersey Transit's Princeton Branch is known as the Dinky Line and is the shortest scheduled train in the United States.

An **elevated train** runs on tracks above the street. Atlanta, Baltimore, Chicago, Los Angeles, Miami, New York, Philadelphia, San Francisco, and Washington, DC, all have elevated train tracks.

A **freight train** has many cars pulled by one or more locomotives. Freight trains transport cargo, not people.

The **Glacier Express** moves slowly—only about 23 miles per hour. This Swiss train passes beautiful mountain views, goes through 91 tunnels, and crosses 291 bridges.

To get on the **Hurricane Turn** in Alaska, riders must wave a white flag to stop the train. When they want to get off, they tell the conductor which milepost to stop at.

An **incline train** travels up a steep railway by means of a cable system. The Lookout Mountain Incline Railway in Tennessee has a 72.7 percent grade near the top—it's one of the world's steepest railways.

AB CD EF GHI JKL MN OP

The **Jupiter** had a cone-shaped chimney called a balloon stack. The train was part of the Golden Spike ceremony in Utah in 1869, celebrating the joining of the Union Pacific and Central Pacific railroad tracks.

The **Komet** runs overnight between Germany and Switzerland. Like a comet in the sky, the train travels at high speed.

The **Leonardo Express** travels back and forth from the airport in Rome, Italy, to the central train station in the city. The trip is just 30 minutes.

A **monorail** train is wider than the one rail it rides on. Monorails can run at ground level, on elevated tracks, or below ground in subway tunnels.

A **narrow-gauge train** is smaller than a regular train and uses narrower tracks. ("Gauge" is the word for the spacing between rails.)

An **ore train** is a freight train that hauls iron ore from mines. It is longer and heavier than most other trains.

Amtrak's **Pacific Surfliner** travels the Southern California coast. It provides a view of palm trees, beaches, and ocean and also has special racks for bikes and surfboards.

The **Q train**'s route is shown in yellow on the New York City subway map. The NYC subway has 24 different train lines and 468 stations.

The **Rocky Mountaineer** passes scenic views of the Canadian Rocky Mountains. It travels from the sea in Vancouver to the mountains in Whistler, British Columbia.

A **snowplow train** clears the snow off railroad tracks. It has rotating, circular blades that carve through the snow, which passes through a chute and is blown to one side of the track.

A **top-and-tail train** has a locomotive at each end so it can easily switch directions. Only the leading locomotive provides the power for the train.

A **unit train** is a freight train that carries only one type of item. Unit train cars stay together from the start to the finish of a trip, which reduces shipping time and cost.

The **Victoria Express** travels between Hanoi and Lào Cai in Vietnam. It includes a dining car and two air-conditioned sleeping cars.

Wilderness trains allow passengers to view the natural world. Arizona's Verde Canyon wilderness train travels past Native American ruins, rock formations, and wildlife— sometimes even bald and golden eagles!

The **Xplorer** is a passenger train in New South Wales, Australia. It links Sydney to Australia's capital, Canberra.

France's **Yellow Train** opened in 1903. The train travels through the Pyrenees Mountains across high bridges, up steep tracks, and through tunnels.

The **California Zephyr** is a passenger train that runs along Amtrak's longest route. It crosses seven states: Illinois, Iowa, Nebraska, Colorado, Utah, Nevada, and California.

First paperback edition 2019
Text copyright © 2015 by Samantha R. Vamos
Illustrations copyright © 2015 by Ryan O'Rourke

Published by Charlesbridge
9 Galen Street
Watertown, MA 02472
(617) 926-0329
www.charlesbridge.com

Library of Congress Cataloging-in-Publication Data
Vamos, Samantha R., author.
    Alphabet trains/Samantha R. Vamos; illustrated by Ryan O'Rourke.
        pages cm
    Summary: Simple text teaches children about different trains and the
alphabet.
    ISBN 978-1-58089-592-7 (reinforced for library use)
    ISBN 978-1-58089-593-4 (softcover)
    ISBN 978-1-60734-857-3 (ebook)
    ISBN 978-1-60734-858-0 (ebook pdf)
1. Railroad trains—Juvenile fiction. 2. English language—Alphabet—
Juvenile fiction. 3. Alphabet books. [1. Stories in rhyme. 2. Railroad trains—
Fiction. 3. Alphabet.] I. O'Rourke, Ryan, illustrator. II. Title.

PZ8.3.V32537Aln 2015
[E]—dc23   2014010487

Printed in China
(hc) 10 9 8 7 6 5 4 3 2 1
(sc) 10 9 8 7 6 5 4 3 2

Illustrations done in Adobe Photoshop
Display type set in Chaloops by Chank Co.
Text type set in Jesterday by Tjarda Koster—Jelloween
Color separations by Colourscan Print Co Pte Ltd, Singapore
Printed by 1010 Printing International Limited in Huizhou, Guangdong, China
Production supervision by Brian G. Walker
Designed by Diane M. Earley

For my sister, Jennifer Sorce.
For Margo Fowler, with gratitude.
And love always to Jackson.
—S. R. V.

For Kaylee.
—R. O.